The Best Brunch Ever

by Carmel Reilly
illustrated by Tom Jellett

"Dad went up the street," said Marcos. "I can cook brunch now!"

Marcos got a spoon and a pan.
He took out eggs and milk.

Marcos mixed the flapjacks.

Mum splashed oil in the pan.

Soon, they had cooked ten plump flapjacks.

Spring looked up at them.

"Quick, Dad will be back soon!" called Mum. "Help me with the card."

Marcos went to jot in the card.

“What was that?” screeched Mum.

Marcos sprang up. He ran to the bench. Spring was scoffing the flapjacks.

“Stop, Spring!” yelled Marcos. “Put the flapjacks down and scram!”

"Dad will be back soon," wailed Marcos. "And not a scrap is left!"

"Do not stress, Marcos," said Mum. "Check the shelf. We still have lots of food."

Mum got a bucket and brush.

“I will fix this mess up,” said Mum.

“You were right, Mum,” said Marcos. “I got a lot of things.”

Dad got back from his run.

“A card and brunch too!” he said.

"Banana splits!" said Dad.
"This is the best brunch ever!"

Look Back

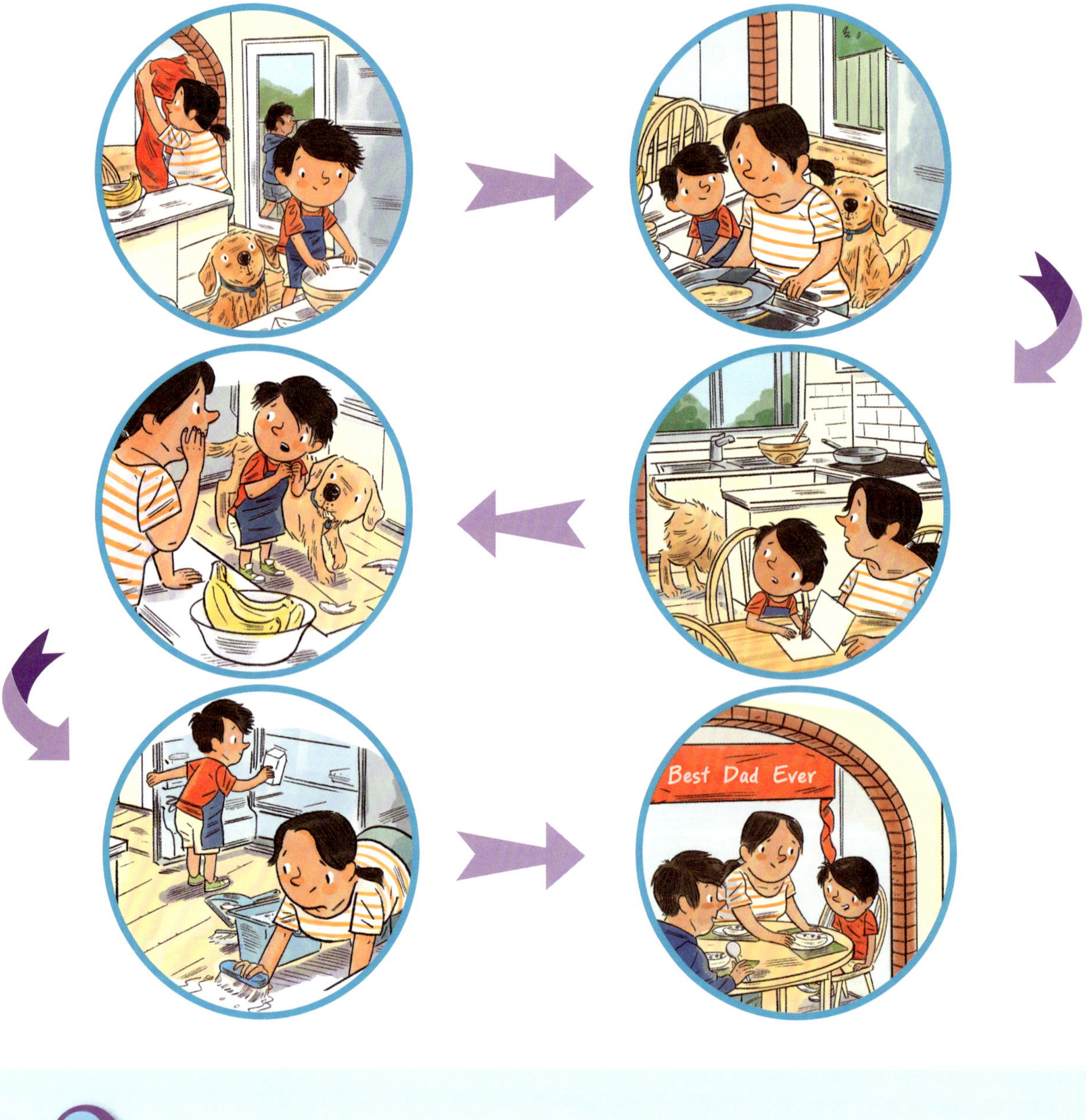

Best Dad Ever

Encourage students to use the pictures to retell the story.